Mother and Son Journal

Pass Back and Forth

How to use this Journal

This mom and son Journal is aimed at knowing each other in the best possible manner. There are no rules as to fill the questions asked. You are free to right in your own words for a keepsake.

This is a pass back and forth kind of journal consisting of prompts on each page to answer. Have fun knowing each other. Use this as a keepsake to have a look at this in future years.

THIS
JOURNAL
belongs to

_____

&

_____

Start Date:

__/ __/ ____

PHOTO OF

You ❤ & *me*

Our Little Story Together!

Dear Mom

Things you love about me?

Dear Son

Things you love about me?

ᮥ·· Dear Mom ·ᮥ

The first thing you say to me in the morning is

~·· Dear Son ··~

The first thing you say to me in the morning is

Dear Mom

What are your goals for this year?

~ ·· Dear Son ·· ~

What are your goals for this year?

·Dear Mom·

What are the things you are grateful for?

Dear Son

What are the things you are grateful for?

~·Dear Mom·~

Your favourite thing to do all day?

Dear Son

your favourite thing to do all day?

~·Dear Mom·~

What's your favourite quote?

Dear Son

What's your favourite quote?

~·Dear Mom·~

What makes you feel better about yourself?

·· Dear Son ··

What makes you feel better about yourself?

Dear Mom

What's your favourite memory with me?

Dear Son

What's your favourite memory with me?

Dear Mom

Describe your dream vacation..

Dear Son

Describe your dream vacation..

~·Dear Mom·~

If you could be invisible for one day what would you do?

~··Dear Son··~

If you could be invisible for one day what would you do?

~ Dear Mom ~

What is your favourite word? Why?

Dear Son

What is your favourite word? Why?

Dear Mom

What is the funniest joke you know?

Dear Son

What is the funniest joke you know?

Dear Mom

Who is the coolest person you've ever met?

Dear Son

Who is the coolest person you've ever met?

Dear Mom

When do you feel the bravest?

~··Dear Son··~

When do you feel the bravest?

Dear Mom

What are you most scared of?

Dear Son

What are you most scared of?

~•Dear Mom•~

What is your favourite season? What do you love about it?

Dear Son

What is your favourite season? What do you love about it?

Dear Mom

What is your favourite kind of food?

Dear Son

What is your favourite kind of food?

Dear Mom

What kind of things make you feel cared for?

Dear Son

What kind of things make you feel cared for?

Dear Mom

What would you like to talk about?

Dear Son

What would you like to talk about?

Dear Mom

What makes you laugh?

Dear Son

What makes you laugh?

~·Dear Mom·~

What are the things that make you angry?

~··Dear Son··~

What are the things that make you angry?

Dear Mom

What is your biggest regret?

~··Dear Son··~

What is your biggest regret?

~·Dear Mom·~

What are you proud of?

Dear Son

What are you proud of?

~ Dear Mom ~

What's your favourite homemade meal?

·· Dear Son ··

What's your favourite homemade meal?

Dear Mom

What makes you feel happy?

Dear Son

What makes you feel happy?

Dear Mom

Describe your perfect day.

Dear Son

Describe your perfect day.

Dear Mom

What's your favourite movie of all time? Why?

Dear Son

What's your favourite movie of all time? Why?

Dear Mom

What are the five things you wish I knew about you?

Dear Son

What are the five things you wish I knew about you?

_____

_____

_____

_____

_____

_____

_____

Dear Mom

What superpower do you already have?

Dear Son

What superpower do you already have?

Dear Mom

What is the best gift you have ever gotten?

Dear Son

What is the best gift you have ever gotten?

~·Dear Mom·~

How do you feel about brothers and sisters?

Dear Son

How do you feel about brothers and sisters?

Dear Mom

Which famous person would you like to meet?

Dear Son

Which famous person would you like to meet?

Dear Mom

What is the one thing you couldn't live without?

Dear Son

What is the one thing you couldn't live without?

Dear Mom

What's your all time favourite song?

Dear Son

What's your all time favourite song?

~ Dear Mom ~

Who do you admire and why?

Dear Son

Who do you admire and why?

~ Dear Mom ~

What's your dream birthday gift?

Dear Son

What's your dream birthday gift?

Dear Mom

When you are sad how
do you make yourself
feel better?

Dear Son

When you are sad how do you make yourself feel better?

Dear Mom

What is your favourite thing about yourself?

Dear Son

What is your favourite thing about yourself?

Dear Mom

Do you prefer cake or ice cream?

Dear Son

Do you prefer cake or ice cream?

~·Dear Mom·~

What is the silliest thing you have ever done?

Dear Son

What is the silliest thing you have ever done?

Dear Mom

What is something that embarasses you alot?

Dear Mom

What is something that embarasses you alot?

Dear Mom

What is something you look for in a friend?

Dear Son

What is something you look for in a friend?

Dear Mom

What is something that really confuses you?

Dear Son

What is something that really confuses you?

~·Dear Mom·~

What do you remember most about the past year?

Dear Son

What do you remember most about the past year?

Dear Mom

What is it that you learned from me?

Dear Son

What is it that you learned from me?

Dear Mom

What is it that you dont want me to forget?

Dear Son

What is it that you dont want me to forget?

Dear Mom

Thank you for.....

Dear Son

Thank you for.....

We have reached the end!

End Date:

__/ __/ ____

One word which describes my mom the best ....

One word which describes my son the best ....

.

Printed in Great Britain
by Amazon

51898722R00057